The Sense of Taste

ELLEN WEISS

WITHDRAWN

Children's Press®
An Imprint of Scholastic Inc.
New York Toronto London Auckland Sydney
Mexico City New Delhi Hong Kong
Danbury, Connecticut

Content Consultant
Lawrence J. Cheskin, M.D.
Johns Hopkins Bloomberg School of Public Health
Baltimore, MD

Library of Congress Cataloging-in-Publication Data

Weiss, Ellen.
  The sense of taste / by Ellen Weiss.
      p. cm. -- (A true book)
  Includes index.
      ISBN-13: 978-0-531-16873-8 (lib. bdg.)
                978-0-531-21835-8 (pbk.)
      ISBN-10: 0-531-16873-5 (lib. bdg.)
                0-531-21835-X (pbk.)

1. Taste--Juvenile literature. I. Title.

  QP456.W45 2008
  612.8'7--dc22   2007048083

Produced by Weldon Owen Education Inc.

1 2 3 4 5 6 7 8 9 10 R 18 17 16 15 14 13 12 11 10 09

Find the Truth!

Everything you are about to read is true *except* for one of the sentences on this page.

Which one is **TRUE**?

T or F   Your tongue is a bundle of muscles.

T or F   Chili peppers have a very strong taste.

Find the answers in this book.

Contents

THE **BIG** TRUTH!

Supertaster!

Christopher Columbus was the first European to taste cocoa.

Milk needs to be kept refrigerated to stay fresh and taste good.

CHAPTER 1

A Taste-Filled Life

Taste lends flavor to eating and to life. It helps make eating fun. Imagine going through life with no sense of taste. Without taste, you wouldn't understand the meaning of *delicious*. You also wouldn't know if milk was spoiled. You would have to hope that someone would cry out, "Don't drink it! It's gone bad." Without the warning, you could make yourself sick.

Taste often helps protect you from swallowing food or drink that's gone bad.

Important Information

Taste, along with sight, hearing, touch, and smell, gives you information about your surroundings. The information from taste is important. It tells you what you are eating, drinking, and swallowing. The information could be, "Yes, that's healthy; I'll finish eating it," or "Get that out of my mouth right now—it's not good!"

Food that makes you sick might not taste bad. Meat, milk products, and eggs are among the foods that can make you sick if they are too old or have been left in the sun.

If you have a good
time when eating
or preparing a
specific food, you'll
probably remember
it and feel good
about that food.

Feelings and Food

Our sense of taste is closely related to our sense of smell. The mouth and nose connect, and so do tastes and smells. That's why you may dislike the smell of a certain food if you once became sick after eating it. In fact, more than half of what we think of as taste is actually sense information received as smell!

9

Our tongues help us eat many foods, including lollipops.

CHAPTER 2

The Terrific Tongue

Your tongue is a bundle of muscles attached to a bone way back in your head, at the base of your skull. Your tongue has an amazing ability to move. For example, your tongue can move food from the front of your mouth to the back before you swallow it. Of course, your tongue has another great skill—tasting. Those tiny bumps on your tongue hold the key to discovering what's yummy or yucky.

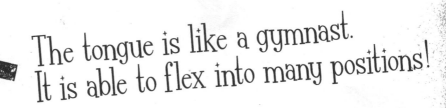

The tongue is like a gymnast. It is able to flex into many positions!

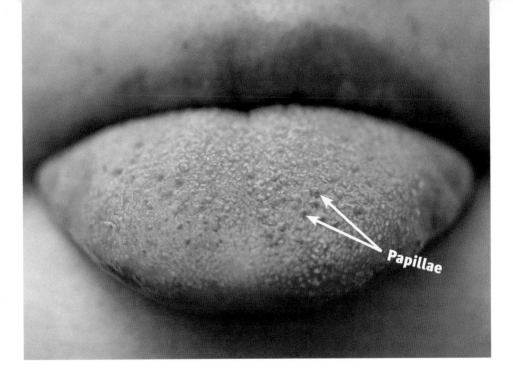

Papillae

Tiny Red Spots

You might have heard that the bumps on the surface of your tongue are your taste buds. That's not correct. Taste buds are so tiny that they can be seen only with a microscope. They are packed into things called **papillae** (puh-PIL-ee). The papillae are those bumps on your tongue. We also have taste buds in other parts of the mouth and throat. There are some on the roof of the mouth, for example.

Babies' Bumps

Babies have more papillae than children or adults. Newborns have many taste buds all over their cheeks and the roofs of their mouths, as well as on their tongues. That might be why babies often don't like foods with strong flavors. As people get older, they have fewer taste buds. The taste buds are less sensitive, too.

Babies have a strong sense of taste. They do not need added sugar or salt.

Inside the Papillae

Papillae are spread out all over your tongue. Not all papillae have taste buds. However, a papilla that has taste buds may have as many as 200! In each taste bud, there are 50 to 100 **receptor cells**. These cells pick up a taste's chemical message. They also change that chemical message to an electrical one.

The Four Types of Papillae

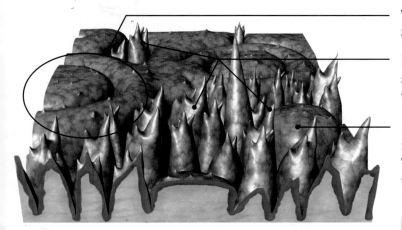

Vallate: Most people have 8 to 12 of these.

Filiform: These are the smallest and most numerous type. They have no taste buds.

Fungiform: These are mushroom-shaped. They are often near the tip of the tongue.

Foliated: These can sometimes be seen without a microscope on children's tongues. They look like horizontal lines.

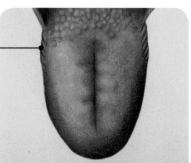

Electrical Taste Signals

Electrical signals from receptor cells travel along nerves to taste areas in your brain. Some signals go to the brain's **cortex**. There they become information about what taste you're sensing. Other signals go to brain areas linked to feelings and memory. Those signals turn a simple taste into something with emotional associations that may last for years.

Pathways to the Brain

Taste center

Cortex

Olfactory (smell) center

Nerves from tongue and taste buds

Nostrils for smelling

Tongue, taste buds, and receptor cells

Salivary glands (make saliva)

Breaking Down Food

The food we eat is made up of tiny particles called **molecules**. Molecules are the building blocks of everything around us, including everything we eat. When you take a bite of any food, you begin the process of breaking it down. Chewing it with your teeth grinds it up. These smaller pieces dissolve in your saliva. Finally, individual food molecules come into contact with taste receptor cells. The cells send signals to your brain.

When you think you're about to eat, your mouth produces more saliva to prepare for it.

Flavor Is Born

Your brain can't "taste" something sweet, but it recognizes the electrical signals that say "sweet." These taste signals are only one part of the picture, however. In the brain's cortex, taste signals interact with touch and smell signals to create our awareness of flavor. Our sense of touch tells us whether a food is mushy, crunchy, hot, or cold, for example. Memory and emotions also contribute to our idea of flavor.

People often hold their noses to keep them from picking up the smell part of taste.

17

Bye-Bye, Buds

There are times when you lose your sense of taste and your awareness of flavor. This often happens when you get a cold. If your nose is blocked, your sense of smell can't work with your taste buds to taste some foods. When your nose becomes unblocked, you are able to enjoy your food again.

Another way to lose your sense of taste is to put burning hot food in your mouth. When your

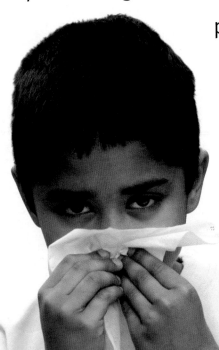

papillae get burned, it takes them a couple of days to recover. Until then, you may not be able to taste your food properly.

Eating a variety of foods can increase your interest in different tastes. Mixing ingredients also varies your intake of nutrients.

Kelp, or kombu, is a type of seaweed often used in cooking. About 100 years ago, scientist Kikunae Ikeda set out to discover what made it so delicious. He found a chemical called glutamate. He called its taste "umami."

CHAPTER 3

The Five Tastes

Scientists used to think that there were only four tastes: bitter, sweet, sour, and salty. However, many now believe that we can sense five tastes. The fifth taste is called umami (ooh-MAH-mee). A Japanese chemist was the first to describe umami. It is said to be a meat-like or savory taste.

You can taste umami in kelp, fish, tomatoes, meat, beans, grains, and many other foods.

Bitter Taste

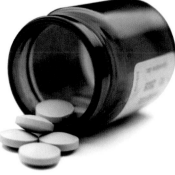

There are good reasons why we like and dislike different tastes. Most people don't like things that taste very bitter. That may be because poisons are often bitter. Have you ever swallowed a pill that tasted bad? It was probably bitter. In large quantities, it may have been poisonous.

Sometimes foods that are only a little bitter are very good for you. These include broccoli, spinach, and Brussels sprouts.

Broccoli

Brussels sprouts

Spinach

Sweet and Sour

Many people like sweet foods. Sweet foods often contain sugar, a type of **carbohydrate**. Carbohydrates give us the energy we need to carry out our daily activities. Fruits, vegetables, and whole grains are healthy carbohydrate choices. Candy and soft drinks are less healthy.

Some sour foods help our bodies absorb minerals. We often don't like foods that are very sour, because they can be **acidic**. Too much acid can upset your digestion.

Foods that are sour include citrus fruits, such as lemons and grapefruits.

Salt Taste

Most animals, including humans, need salt. Salt helps the body's cells work properly. In the wild, many animals lick salt deposits wherever they find them. However, too much salt may be bad for you. It can lead to problems with your heart and kidneys. Many people are careful about the amount of salt they add to their food.

These red and green macaws from the Amazon jungle are licking salty clay.

24

Truly Tasteless

Some people mistakenly believe that the "hot" sensation you get from chili peppers is a kind of taste. In fact, the chemical that makes peppers hot—capsaicin (kap-SAY-uh-sin)—has no taste. Instead, capsaicin works with pain receptors in your taste buds. A message of pain is sent to your brain. However, chili peppers aren't bad for you. You just have to be careful when you're eating them. They can make it difficult for you to taste other things for a while!

Step 1

Swab some of the food coloring onto the tip of your tongue. The tongue will turn blue except for some pink spots. These pink spots are your papillae.

Step 2

Put the piece of paper onto the tip of the tongue. Using the magnifying glass, count how many pink dots are inside the hole.

Nontaster

If you have fewer than 15 papillae, you are a nontaster.

Taster

If you have between 15 and 35 papillae, you are an average taster.

Supertaster

If you have more than 35 papillae, you are a supertaster.

Supertaster!

Are you a picky eater? If you are, it may be because you're a supertaster. About a quarter of all people have an extra-excellent sense of taste. These people have more than twice as many taste buds as normal.

What kind of taster are you? To find out, you will need some blue food coloring. You will also need a magnifying glass and a piece of paper with a quarter-inch (7-millimeter) hole punched through it.

Smell helps us test the flavor of a food before we even put it in our mouths.

CHAPTER 4

Testing Taste

Using only our taste buds, we experience the five basic tastes of salty, bitter, sour, sweet, and umami in foods. However, our sense of smell helps us tell the difference between many foods that might otherwise taste almost the same, such as cabbage and broccoli. Our other senses—even sight—also add to our experience of taste.

Your nose can pick up as many as 10,000 different smells.

Fool Your Brain

Your brain is good at detecting flavors, but it can be fooled. Here's an experiment to try with a few friends. Get some soda in two different flavors, such as grape and lime. Get a bottle of seltzer or club soda too. Put some orange food coloring into the seltzer or soda. It will turn orange, like orange soda. (The food coloring will change only the color of the soda, not the taste.)

Then pour some of each kind of soda into glasses. Tell your friends to taste each one, but don't tell them the orange soda is a fake. How many think that the orange-colored one is orange-flavored soda?

People often think
a product tastes better
if the color looks good.
Food manufacturers
know all about this.
That's why so many
foods contain
artificial coloring.

Gelato
Noix de Coco

Gelato
Framboise

Taste Testers

Supertasters experience flavor more intensely than most other people. Most supertasters are women, because women often have a sharper sense of taste than men. Some supertasters earn money from their tasting skills. Food manufacturers hire these experts to try different foods before the foods are made in large quantities. The tasters test for taste, texture, and smell—the ingredients of flavor!

Professional tasters may have to spend a lot of time trying foods they don't like.

Smelly Fruit

Most things we eat either smell good and taste good, or smell bad and taste bad. But there are some exceptions.

Meet the durian fruit. It's about as big as a bowling ball. It grows in Southeast Asia. Inside its tough, spiky shell is a fruit that smells disgusting—at least to people who have yet to taste the fruit! The durian is said to smell as if someone nearby has had bad stomach trouble. But, strangely, if you can get past the smell, many say the fruit tastes delicious.

This woman is preparing food for a stall in a Vietnamese market in Southeast Asia. The herbs lemongrass and mint are often added to Vietnamese food.

CHAPTER 5

Flavors in Our Lives

People's preferences for certain foods have affected history. For centuries, merchants crossed enormous stretches of land and sea. They traded in salt, spices, and herbs. Trends in eating and drinking play a part in the behavior, habits, customs, and jobs of people everywhere. Food is an important "ingredient" in the world's economy.

About 500 years ago, spices sent to Europe from southeastern Asia were worth about the same as gold powder.

Herbs and Spices

For thousands of years, people have added herbs and spices to their food to make it more flavorful. Herbs and spices come from plants. Herbs usually come from leaves, used fresh or dried. Basil, oregano, chives, and parsley are commonly used herbs. Spices usually come from bark, roots, flowers, fruits, or seeds. They are usually dried or ground into a powder. Cinnamon, cloves, black pepper, mustard, and nutmeg are spices.

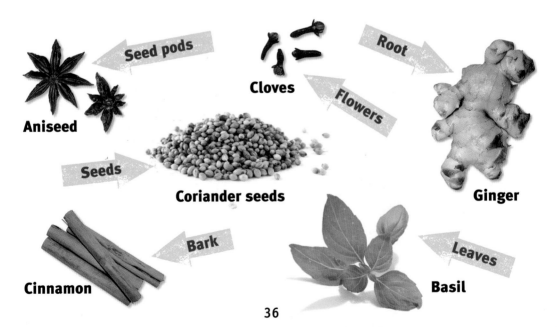

Seed pods

Aniseed

Cloves

Root

Flowers

Seeds

Coriander seeds

Ginger

Bark

Cinnamon

Leaves

Basil

Saffron is the most expensive spice. It takes 60,000 flowers to make one pound!

In ancient times, herbs and spices were rare and precious. Most spices came from East Asia. Europeans were eager for cinnamon, cloves, and other spices to flavor and preserve their food. Spices were transported from East Asia to western Asia and Europe along the Spice Route. This was a network of sea routes. The routes went around the southern tip of India.

As time passed, western European countries wanted a faster sea route to East Asia. When Christopher Columbus came upon America in 1492, he was actually being paid by the Spanish to find a more direct sea route to India!

Copying Nature

Today, people don't need natural ingredients in order to change the taste of foods. About 50 years ago, some scientists asked: "What makes a raspberry taste like a raspberry?" They set out to discover the chemical makeup of the raspberry taste. Once they found the molecule, they were able to reproduce the flavor in a laboratory. That's how the chemical-flavor industry was born.

Scientists who develop flavors are called flavorists. They need to find chemicals that last a long time and still taste good.

Flavor companies can now make seemingly endless flavors. They can produce the flavor of a red or black raspberry, or a raspberry from California. They have several hundred varieties of strawberry flavor.

This scientist has added a human-made strawberry flavor to cow's milk.

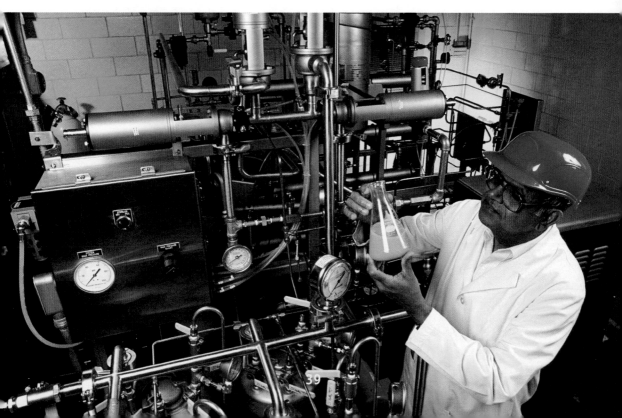

International Superstars

In the world of flavors, chocolate and vanilla are undoubtedly the superstars. Their popularity shows that people will go to great lengths for a food they find delicious.

Vanilla and chocolate were first used as foods hundreds of years ago, in Central and South America. Vanilla comes from the dried pods of a vine. Chocolate comes from the seeds of the cacao tree. Originally, the drink made from chocolate was a bitter one. Chili and vanilla were sometimes added, but sugar was not.

Chocolate Time Line

250 A.D.
Ancient Mayans use cacao to make a bitter drink.

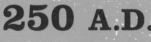

1400 A.D.
Ancient Aztecs use cacao seeds for money. Chocolate is drunk mostly by royalty and priests.

Chocolate drink was introduced to Europe in the 1500s. Europeans added vanilla to the drink, as well as sugar and milk to sweeten it. Vanilla was also new to Europeans. It became a big hit. People soon realized that it had a wonderful fragrance as well as taste. People started using it in perfumes.

Today, the world's appetite for chocolate and vanilla is as strong as ever. One study has found that the average American eats approximately 10,000 chocolate bars in his or her lifetime!

1521 A.D.

Spain conquers the Aztecs. Chocolate is sent back to Spain. Sugar is added to it for the first time.

1828 A.D.

The cocoa press is invented. It is easier to make chocolate. The press crushes cocoa beans, separating the cocoa butter from the rest of the bean.

Taste Into the Future

The world's fascination with— and craving for—flavors is likely to continue. Scientists are still studying taste and how it works in our bodies. People's bodies vary, so our tastes do too. Our feelings about taste, often attached to memories, also change.

However, one constant is the importance of taste. It leads us to good food and even keeps us safe! ★

Chinese cuisine **is famous for its variety of flavors.**

True Statistics

Amount of saliva you can make in a lifetime: About 10,000 gallons (37,854 liters). That is enough to fill a swimming pool!

Number of chemical compounds in a simple natural flavor: About 200

Number of chemical compounds in a more complicated flavor: As many as 6,000

Average number of taste buds in humans: About 10,000

Percentage of people who are nontasters: About 25 percent

Did you find the truth?

T Your tongue is a bundle of muscles.

F Chili peppers have a very strong taste.

Resources

Books

Cobb, Vicki. *How to Really Fool Yourself: Illusions for All Your Senses*. Hoboken, NJ: Jossey-Bass, 1999.

Frost, Helen. *Tasting* (The Senses). Mankato, MN: Capstone Press, 1999.

Making Sense of Senses (Experiment With Science). Danbury, CT: Children's Press, 2007.

Pringle, Laurence P. *Taste* (Explore Your Senses). New York: Benchmark Books, 1999.

Pryor, Kimberley Jane. *Tasting* (Senses). New York: Chelsea Clubhouse, 2003.

Silverstein, Alvin and Virginia, and Silverstein Nunn, Laura. *Smelling and Tasting* (Senses and Sensors). Brookfield, CT: Twenty-First Century Books, 2002.

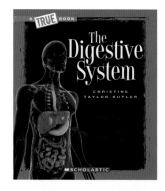

Taylor-Butler, Christine. *The Digestive System* (A True Book: Health and the Human Body). Danbury, CT: Children's Press, 2008.

Organizations and Web Sites

Neuroscience for Kids
http://faculty.washington.edu/chudler/tasty.html
Read some tongue and taste facts, and try experiments to test your sense of taste.

ThinkQuest
http://library.thinkquest.org/3750/taste/taste.html
Test your knowledge by answering quiz questions about the senses.

Places to Visit

Chocolate Exhibition
The Field Museum
1440 S. Lake Shore Dr
Chicago, IL 60605-2496
(312) 922 9410
www.fieldmuseum.org/chocolate/index.html
This mouth-watering exhibit tours the country. Click on "chocolate tour" to see where it is now.

Idaho Potato Museum
Highway 91
Blackfoot, ID 83221
(208) 785 2517
www.potatoexpo.com
Learn everything about the potato industry and how to cook tasty potatoes. Find out who made the world's largest potato chip!

Important Words

acidic (uh-SID-ik) – relating to the sour taste that some substances have

carbohydrate (kar-boh-HYE-drate) – a nutrient in food, which the body converts to glucose

cortex (KOR-teks) – the outer layer of an internal organ, such as the brain

cuisine (kwi-ZEEN) – a way or style of preparing and cooking food

molecule (MOL-uh-kyool) – the smallest part of a substance that displays all the chemical properties of that substance

papilla (puh-PIL-uh) – a tiny bump on the tongue, on which taste buds may be located

receptor cell (re-SEP-tur SEL) – a cell in the body that is affected by the chemicals in food. It sends an electrical signal to the brain, telling your brain what you are tasting.

saliva (suh-LYE-vuh) – the clear liquid in your mouth that helps you swallow and helps your body start breaking down food

Index

Page numbers in **bold** indicate illustrations.

About the Author

Ellen Weiss went to Oberlin College and Columbia University. She has written more than 200 books, both fiction and nonfiction, for children of all ages. She has also written songs and created videos for kids. Her work has won a Grammy Award, a Parents' Choice Award, and three Children's Choice Awards. She and her husband, Mel Friedman, live in New York City. They often collaborate on books. The Disney Channel adapted one of their books, *The Poof Point*, for a television movie.

PHOTOGRAPHS: Amy Lam (tongue, p. 14); Big Stock Photo (p. 4; p. 21; pill bottle, p 22; p. 33; coriander seeds, p. 36; p. 38); Getty Images (front cover; p. 6; p. 9; close-up of papillae, p. 14; p. 16; p. 19; p. 28; p. 42); iStockphoto.com (© Andrey Shchekalev, back cover; © Adrian Costea, p. 12; © Arvind Balaraman, p. 18; © Damir Spanic, p. 31; © Donna Coleman, p. 23; © Kirill Zdorov, p. 13; © Philip Dyer, p. 10; p. 5; p. 8; p. 30; cacao beans, p. 40; p. 43); Photolibrary (p. 17; p. 20; p. 24; pp. 26–27; p. 34; p. 39); PhotoNewZealand (Javier Larrea, p. 32); Stock.Xchng (basil, p. 36; p. 37; powdered chocolate, p. 41); Stockxpert (p. 3); Tranz/Corbis (p. 25)